ORION BIT

AI Agents Vs Workflows

Understanding the Difference in Automation

Contents

1

Introduction to AI Agents and Workflows

Artificial Intelligence (AI) is transforming how we approach automation, offering tools and systems that streamline tasks and enhance efficiency. Two concepts frequently arise in this domain: **AI agents** and **workflows**. While both contribute to automation, they differ significantly in their design, capabilities, and applications. Yet, confusion between the two persists, fueled by marketing buzz and overlapping outcomes. This book seeks to untangle these concepts, providing clarity on what sets AI agents apart from workflows and why that distinction matters.

In this chapter, we will define AI agents and workflows that use AI Large Language Model (LLM) APIs, examine the reasons behind their frequent conflation, and underline the practical and theoretical importance of understanding their differences. We'll conclude with an overview of the book's structure to guide you through the journey ahead.

What is an AI Agent?

An **AI agent** is an autonomous entity designed to perceive its environment, make decisions, and take actions to achieve specific goals. Unlike traditional software that rigidly follows a script, AI agents operate with a level of independence, adapting to changes and uncertainties in their surroundings. Their key characteristics include:

- **Autonomy**: AI agents function without constant human oversight, relying on their own decision-making processes.
- **Perception**: They gather and interpret data from their environment—be it physical, digital, or a blend of both.
- **Decision-Making**: Using reasoning, learning, or planning, they determine the best course of action to meet their objectives.
- **Action**: They actively interact with their environment, effecting change to accomplish their goals.

A classic example is a **self-driving car**. Equipped with sensors like cameras and lidar, it perceives road conditions, traffic signals, and obstacles. It decides when to turn, speed up, or stop, and then acts by controlling the vehicle—all to safely reach its destination. This adaptability to real-time changes distinguishes it as an AI agent.

Other examples include:

- **Robotic vacuum cleaners** that map a room and clean autonomously.
- **Trading bots** that analyze market trends and execute trades.
- **Virtual assistants** that evolve based on user interactions to

offer tailored suggestions.

What is a Workflow Using AI LLM APIs?

A **workflow** is a structured sequence of tasks engineered to produce a specific result. When paired with **AI LLM APIs** (e.g., GPT, BERT), workflows leverage advanced language models to perform functions like text generation or data analysis. However, they lack the autonomy of AI agents, adhering to a predefined script rather than making independent decisions.

Consider a **customer service system**:

1. A user submits a question.
2. An AI model classifies the query's intent.
3. The system routes it to the relevant department.
4. An AI-generated response is delivered.

Here, the AI LLM API enhances the workflow by crafting natural-language responses, but the process itself is fixed. If an unexpected scenario arises, the system can't deviate from its path without human reprogramming.

Additional examples include:

- **Content generation pipelines** that produce reports from data inputs.
- **Sentiment analysis workflows** that process social media posts in a set order.
- **Scripted chatbots** that rely on AI for replies but follow a rigid structure.

Unlike AI agents, workflows excel in predictable, repetitive contexts where the steps are well-defined.

Why Does Confusion Exist?

Despite their differences, AI agents and workflows are often mistaken for one another. Several factors drive this confusion:

- **Marketing Hype**: Businesses may label a workflow as an "AI agent" to suggest cutting-edge sophistication, even if it lacks autonomy. This inflates perceptions and obscures the truth.
- **Superficial Similarities**: Both systems automate tasks, yielding comparable results on the surface. A self-driving car and an automated support chatbot both reduce human effort, but their inner workings diverge sharply.
- **Loose Terminology**: The word "agent" is sometimes applied to any task-performing software, diluting its technical meaning.
- **Overhyped AI Capabilities**: Advances in LLMs lead some to assume any AI-powered system is autonomous, overlooking the scripted nature of workflows.

This muddled perception can mislead users, skewing expectations and technology choices.

Importance of Distinguishing Between Them

Clarifying the distinction between AI agents and workflows carries significant weight, both practically and theoretically:

Practical Reasons

- **Right Tool for the Job**: AI agents suit tasks requiring adaptability—like robotics or dynamic decision-making—while workflows shine in structured, repeatable scenarios like data processing. Misjudging this can derail projects.
- **Efficiency and Cost**: Building an AI agent demands more resources than a workflow. Using one when the other suffices wastes time and money.
- **Scalability**: Workflows are simpler to scale and maintain due to their predictability, whereas AI agents need ongoing tuning to handle evolving conditions.

Theoretical Reasons

- **Research Clarity**: Differentiating them sharpens focus in AI development, advancing work on autonomy, learning, and ethics.
- **Conceptual Understanding**: It reveals the breadth of AI's role in automation, from basic task execution to complex, self-directed systems.

2

Fundamentals of AI Agents

In Chapter 1, we introduced AI agents as autonomous entities that perceive their environments, make decisions, and act to fulfill specific objectives, distinguishing them from rigid, predefined workflows. Here, we dive deeper into the core concepts that define AI agents: their key properties, the various types that exist, the environments they navigate, and real-world examples that showcase their capabilities. A special focus is placed on their **nondeterministic approach**, which allows them to iteratively refine their actions, correct mistakes, and adapt to challenges—qualities that make them uniquely suited for complex, unpredictable scenarios.

This chapter provides a theoretical foundation for understanding AI agents, preparing us to later compare them with workflow-based systems and explore their practical applications.

Definition and Key Properties of AI Agents

An **AI agent** is a system—software, hardware, or a combination of both—that operates independently within an environment. It perceives its surroundings through sensors or data inputs, processes that information using algorithms, and executes actions via effectors or outputs to achieve predefined goals. Unlike traditional software, which executes a fixed sequence of instructions, AI agents thrive in uncertainty, adapting their behavior to dynamic conditions. Their **nondeterministic nature** means they don't follow a single, predictable path; instead, they can explore multiple strategies, iterating and adjusting their actions until they succeed.

The defining properties of AI agents are:

- **Autonomy**: AI agents function without constant human oversight. They analyze situations, select actions, and refine their behavior based on outcomes. For example, a self-driving car decides its speed and lane position independently, adjusting as traffic conditions change.
- **Reactivity**: Agents continuously sense their environment and respond to changes in real-time. This is critical in dynamic settings—consider a robotic arm that pauses or reposition itself when it detects an obstruction during assembly.
- **Pro activity**: Beyond reacting, AI agents actively pursue goals. They plan and execute sequences of actions to achieve their objectives, such as a virtual assistant scheduling meetings by anticipating user needs and coordinating availability.
- **Social Ability**: Many agents interact with other agents or

humans, collaborating or competing as needed. In a multi-agent system like autonomous drones mapping an area, each drone communicates to avoid collisions and ensure complete coverage.

These properties enable AI agents to excel where rigid systems falter. Their nondeterministic approach—trying, failing, and retrying with adjustments—mirrors how humans solve problems in unpredictable settings, making them invaluable for real-world automation.

Types of AI Agents

AI agents vary in complexity, from basic systems following simple rules to advanced ones that learn and optimize over time. Below, we explore the main types, emphasizing how their designs support goal achievement, especially through iteration and correction.

Simple Reflex Agents (Rule-Based Responses)

Simple reflex agents operate using predefined condition-action rules. They perceive the current state of their environment and instantly act based on a matching rule, without memory or foresight.

- **How They Work**: If condition X is met, perform action Y. No past states are considered.
- **Example**: A smart sprinkler system that activates when soil moisture drops below a threshold.

- **Nondeterminism**: Limited. These agents don't iterate or correct; if a rule fails (e.g., the sprinkler waters a flooded area due to a broken sensor), they lack the capacity to adjust without reprogramming.
- **Use Case**: Ideal for fully observable, static environments with clear, predictable rules.

Model-Based Reflex Agents (Using Internal Models)

Model-based reflex agents enhance simple reflex agents by maintaining an internal model of the world, tracking unobservable aspects of the environment to inform decisions.

- **How They Work**: They combine current percepts with an internal state (e.g., a memory of past actions) to choose actions.
- **Example**: A robotic vacuum cleaner like the Roomba builds a mental map of a room, avoiding cleaned areas and adjusting to new obstacles.
- **Nondeterminism**: Moderate. If the vacuum bumps into furniture, it updates its map and tries a new path, iterating until it covers the space.
- **Use Case**: Suited for partially observable environments where context improves decision-making.

Goal-Based Agents (Pursuing Objectives)

Goal-based agents focus on achieving specific endpoints. They evaluate potential actions based on how they advance toward a goal, often using search or planning algorithms.

- **How They Work**: They simulate future states to select the best action sequence.
- **Example**: A navigation app finding the fastest route to a destination, rerouting if traffic jams arise.
- **Nondeterminism**: High. If a chosen route fails (e.g., a road closure), the agent recalculates and tests alternatives, iterating until it succeeds.
- **Use Case**: Effective in dynamic environments where goals require flexible planning.

Utility-Based Agents (Optimizing Outcomes)

Utility-based agents aim not just to achieve goals but to maximize a measure of success, using a utility function to rank outcomes.

- **How They Work**: They weigh trade-offs (e.g., time vs. cost) to select actions with the highest expected utility.
- **Example**: A stock trading bot balancing profit and risk, adjusting trades based on market shifts.
- **Nondeterminism**: High. If a trade loses money, the bot reevaluates its strategy, retrying with refined parameters to optimize returns.
- **Use Case**: Best for scenarios with multiple successful paths, requiring optimization.

Learning Agents (Adapting Over Time)

Learning agents evolve their behavior through experience, using techniques like machine learning to improve performance.

- **How They Work**: They include a learning component that adjusts their decision-making based on feedback.
- **Example**: A chatbot that refines its responses as it learns user preferences.
- **Nondeterminism**: Very high. These agents use trial-and-error (e.g., reinforcement learning), repeatedly testing actions, assessing results, and correcting mistakes to master tasks.
- **Use Case**: Ideal for complex, stochastic environments where adaptability is key.

Environments in Which AI Agents Operate

The environment shapes an AI agent's design and capabilities. Below are the key dimensions that define these environments, with examples of how agents adapt:

- **Fully Observable vs. Partially Observable**:
- **Fully Observable**: The agent sees everything relevant (e.g., a chess game). Simple reflex agents suffice here.
- **Partially Observable**: Only partial data is available (e.g., a poker game with hidden cards). Model-based or learning agents track unseen elements and iterate to infer the state.
- **Deterministic vs. Stochastic**:
- **Deterministic**: Actions have certain outcomes (e.g., a calculator). Goal-based agents plan reliably here.
- **Stochastic**: Outcomes are uncertain (e.g., weather prediction). Learning agents use probabilistic methods, retrying strategies to handle randomness.

- **Static vs. Dynamic**:
- **Static**: The environment stays constant during deliberation (e.g., a Sudoku puzzle). Simple agents work well.
- **Dynamic**: The environment changes (e.g., a busy highway). Reactive, goal-based agents adjust in real-time.
- **Discrete vs. Continuous**:
- **Discrete**: Finite states/actions (e.g., tic-tac-toe). Utility-based agents optimize efficiently.
- **Continuous**: Infinite possibilities (e.g., robot motion). Learning agents approximate solutions through iteration.
- **Single-Agent vs. Multi-Agent**:
- **Single-Agent**: One agent acts alone (e.g., a thermostat). Any type may suffice.
- **Multi-Agent**: Multiple agents interact (e.g., autonomous cars at an intersection). Social ability and coordination are critical.

Agents must match their environment's complexity. A learning agent in a stochastic, dynamic, multi-agent setting (e.g., swarm robotics) iterates and corrects more than a reflex agent in a static, deterministic one (e.g., a light switch).

The Non Deterministic Nature of AI Agents

A hallmark of AI agents is their **non deterministic approach**, distinguishing them from workflows' linear paths. They don't assume a single correct sequence; instead, they explore, fail, and refine their actions to achieve goals. This is vital in real-world settings where uncertainty reigns.

- **Iterative Refinement**: Goal-based agents exemplify this. A delivery drone facing a blocked path recalculates its route, testing new options until it reaches its destination. Each failure informs the next attempt.
- **Trial and Error**: Learning agents, like those using reinforcement learning, thrive on this. A robotic arm learning to stack blocks might drop them repeatedly, adjusting its grip strength and angle with each try until it succeeds.
- **Handling Uncertainty**: In stochastic environments, utility-based agents use probabilistic models. A weather forecasting agent predicts rain, compares it to actual outcomes, and refines its model over iterations to improve accuracy.

This adaptability—retrying with corrections—mirrors real AI agents' behavior. Unlike workflows, which halt on errors, AI agents persist, making them robust for tasks like autonomous navigation or customer service automation.

Examples of AI Agents

Here are detailed examples showcasing AI agents' diversity and nondeterministic strategies:

Robotic Agents: Autonomous Vacuum Cleaners

- **Description**: Devices like the Roomba use sensors to navigate and clean floors autonomously.
- **Type**: Model-based reflex agent.
- **Environment**: Partially observable (limited sensor range), dynamic (moving obstacles), stochastic (random dirt).

- **Nondeterminism**: If it hits a chair, it adjusts its path, retrying until it cleans the area, updating its internal map with each iteration.

Software Agents: Trading Bots

- **Description**: Bots analyze market data and execute trades to maximize profit.
- **Type**: Utility-based agent.
- **Environment**: Partially observable (incomplete market data), stochastic (price volatility), dynamic (real-time changes).
- **Nondeterminism**: After a losing trade, it refines its algorithm, testing new patterns to optimize returns over multiple cycles.

Multi-Agent Systems: Swarm Robotics

- **Description**: Teams of robots (e.g., drones) collaborate to map terrain or move objects.
- **Type**: Learning agents.
- **Environment**: Partially observable, dynamic, multi-agent (coordination required).
- **Nondeterminism**: If one drone fails to cover its zone, others adapt, redistributing tasks and iterating until the collective goal is met.

These cases highlight how AI agents' ability to iterate and correct ensures success across diverse domains.

3

Understanding Workflows with AI LLM APIs

In the realm of automation, two concepts often come into focus: AI agents and workflows. While the previous chapter explored AI agents—autonomous systems capable of perceiving environments, making decisions, and adapting to achieve goals—this chapter shifts to **workflows**, a distinct approach to automation. Workflows are structured sequences of tasks designed to produce specific, predictable outcomes. With the integration of AI Large Language Model (LLM) APIs, such as those from OpenAI's GPT or Google's BERT, workflows can perform sophisticated functions like generating text or analyzing data. Yet, despite this enhancement, they remain fundamentally different from AI agents.

This chapter defines workflows, examines their design and execution, and showcases their role in automation through tools like **Zapier**, **Make**, and **n8n**. We'll also address a common misconception: why workflows, even when powered by AI, are not AI agents—despite what some may claim when using these popular web apps.

What is a Workflow?

A **workflow** is a predefined, systematic series of tasks or steps executed in a specific order to achieve a consistent result. Think of it as a recipe: each ingredient (task) is added at the right moment, in the right sequence, to produce the desired dish (outcome). Workflows are widely used in business, software development, and data management to automate repetitive or complex processes efficiently.

Key Characteristics of Workflows

- **Structured Sequence**: Every step is explicitly defined, and the progression from one task to the next follows a set path.
- **Conditionality**: Workflows often include "if-then" logic to handle variations (e.g., "If the email contains 'urgent,' escalate it").
- **Automation**: Once configured, workflows run without manual input, triggered by events like a new form submission or email.
- **Determinism**: Given the same inputs and conditions, a workflow always yields the same output—predictability is its strength.

A Simple Example

Consider an e-commerce order-processing workflow:

1. Customer places an order.
2. System checks inventory.
3. If stock is available, payment is processed; if not, the

customer is notified.

4. A confirmation email is sent.
5. The order is shipped.

This process is streamlined and reliable but rigid. If an unexpected issue arises—like a payment glitch not accounted for in the rules—the workflow can't adapt; it either fails or requires human intervention.

Role of AI LLM APIs in Workflows

AI LLM APIs bring advanced language capabilities to workflows, enabling automation of tasks that once demanded human intelligence. These APIs, powered by models like GPT-4 or BERT, can:

- **Generate Text**: Draft emails, articles, or chatbot responses.
- **Classify Data**: Identify sentiment in reviews or categorize support tickets.
- **Translate Languages**: Convert customer inquiries into a support team's native tongue.
- **Summarize Content**: Condense reports or meeting notes.

How They Fit In

In a workflow, an AI LLM API acts as a specialized tool at a specific step. For example, in a customer support workflow:

- A customer submits a query.
- The API analyzes the text to determine its intent (e.g.,

complaint, question).

- The workflow then routes it to the right team or triggers an auto-reply.

The AI enhances the workflow's capabilities, but it doesn't control the process. The workflow remains a scripted sequence, with the API executing a designated task—no more, no less.

Popular Workflow Automation Tools: Zapier, Make, and n8n

Workflow automation has been revolutionized by web-based platforms that make it accessible to both technical and non-technical users. Among the most widely used are **Zapier**, **Make** (formerly Integromat), and **n8n**. These tools excel at connecting apps and services—including LLMs—to automate tasks efficiently.

Zapier

- **Overview**: Zapier is renowned for its simplicity, allowing users to create "Zaps"—workflows that link apps like Gmail, Slack, and Google Sheets.
- **Example**: A Zap might detect a new email, use an LLM API to summarize it, and post the summary to a Slack channel.
- **Strength**: Ease of use and vast app integrations.

Make

- **Overview**: Make offers a visual, drag-and-drop interface for building complex workflows with advanced logic and data handling.
- **Example**: It could pull customer data from a CRM, generate personalized emails via an LLM API, and schedule them for delivery.
- **Strength**: Flexibility for multi-step processes and API integrations.

n8n

- **Overview**: An open-source, self-hosted platform, n8n caters to users who need customization and control.
- **Example**: A developer might use n8n to fetch social media trends, generate content ideas with an LLM, and publish them to WordPress.
- **Strength**: Extensibility and developer-friendly features.

Connecting LLMs

These tools seamlessly integrate with LLM APIs, enabling tasks like automated content creation or query analysis. For instance, a Zapier workflow might use OpenAI's GPT to draft social media posts, while Make could translate customer feedback into multiple languages. This power has made them indispensable for businesses seeking efficiency.

How Workflows Are Designed and Executed

Creating a workflow is a deliberate process that ensures automation aligns with a specific goal. Here's how it works:

1. **Identify the Task**: Pinpoint a repetitive process (e.g., handling support tickets).
2. **Map the Steps**: Outline each task and its order, including conditions (e.g., "If urgent, notify manager").
3. **Choose Tools**: Select apps or APIs—like Zapier and an LLM—for each step.
4. **Set Triggers and Actions**: Define what starts the workflow (trigger) and what happens next (actions).
5. **Test and Deploy**: Run it with test data, tweak as needed, then activate it.

Execution in Action

Once live, a workflow runs automatically. For example:

Trigger: A new form submission arrives.

Actions:

1. An LLM API classifies the submission's intent.
2. The workflow emails the appropriate team.
3. The entry is logged in a spreadsheet.

This process is static—each run follows the same script, with no deviation unless manually altered.

Examples of Workflows in Action

Let's explore three real-world scenarios to see workflows—and tools like Zapier, Make, and n8n—at work.

1. Customer Service Automation (Chatbots)

Workflow:

1. Customer sends a message.
2. Zapier triggers an LLM API to classify intent (e.g., billing issue).
3. If billing, route to finance; otherwise, generate a reply.
4. Log the interaction.

Outcome: Quick responses, but if the query is ambiguous, the workflow might misroute or stall.

2. Content Generation Pipelines

Workflow:

1. Make pulls trending topics from Twitter.
2. An LLM API generates blog drafts.
3. Drafts are sent to an editor via email.
4. Approved posts are published.

Outcome: Streamlined content creation, but poor drafts pass through unless manually caught.

3. Data Processing and Analysis

Workflow:

1. n8n extracts sales data from a database.
2. An LLM summarizes key trends.
3. Results are visualized in a dashboard.

Outcome: Efficient reporting, but it won't adapt to new data patterns without reprogramming.

These examples highlight workflows' strengths—speed and reliability—and their limits—rigidity.

Why Workflows Are Not AI Agents

Despite their power, workflows built with Zapier, Make, or n8n—even when using LLMs—are often mislabeled as AI agents. This confusion is widespread, but workflows and AI agents differ fundamentally.

Key Differences

Autonomy

- **AI Agents**: Act independently, deciding actions based on goals and environment.
- **Workflows**: Follow a fixed script, with no independent decision-making.

Adaptability

- **AI Agents**: Learn and adjust to new situations over time.
- **Workflows**: Remain static, requiring manual updates to change behavior.

Decision-Making

- **AI Agents**: Use reasoning or algorithms to plan and act.
- **Workflows**: Rely on predefined "if-then" rules, not true reasoning.

Handling Uncertainty

- **AI Agents**: Navigate unpredictable scenarios effectively.
- **Workflows**: Falter when faced with unexpected inputs or errors.

Why the Misconception?

- **Marketing Hype**: Tools like Zapier tout "AI-powered automation," blurring lines between workflows and agents.
- **Surface Similarity**: Both can automate tasks, but workflows lack the intelligence beneath the surface.
- **Overstated AI Role**: An LLM generating text in a Zap might seem smart, but it's just a cog in a scripted machine.

For instance, a Make workflow using GPT to draft emails isn't an AI agent—it's a sequence: trigger → generate → send. The LLM doesn't decide *if* or *when* to send; the workflow does.

Limitations of Workflows Compared to AI Agents

Workflows shine in structured settings but falter elsewhere:

- **Inflexibility**: They can't handle scenarios beyond their rules.
- **No Learning**: Past runs don't improve future ones.
- **Complexity Issues**: Scaling to intricate tasks makes them cumbersome.
- **Limited Decisions**: They follow conditions, not reason.

AI agents, conversely, excel in dynamic contexts—like fraud detection or autonomous navigation—where adaptability and learning are key.

4

Comparing AI Agents and Workflow-Based Systems

Automation technologies promise efficiency and scalability, but not all solutions are created equal. AI agents and workflow-based systems represent two divergent paths: one thrives on independence and intelligence, the other on structure and predictability. This chapter examines their differences through the lenses of autonomy, adaptability, and decision-making, offering practical guidance on their applications and dispelling myths that often blur the lines between them. Whether you're designing systems or deploying them, understanding these distinctions is key to unlocking their full potential.

Autonomy: Independent Action vs. Fixed Paths

AI Agents: Masters of Self-Direction

At the heart of an AI agent lies its **autonomy**—the capacity to act without human hand-holding. Equipped with sensors, algorithms, and goals, AI agents analyze their surroundings and decide their next move in real time. This makes them ideal for environments where conditions shift unpredictably.

- **Real-World Example**: Picture an autonomous delivery drone. It doesn't follow a rigid flight plan. Instead, it adjusts its route based on wind speed, obstacles, and no-fly zones, all while ensuring timely delivery. Its decisions are its own, guided by a blend of perception and intent.

Workflows: Executors of Predefined Steps

Workflows, by contrast, are the opposite of autonomous. They operate along a **fixed sequence**, executing tasks as scripted by a human designer. Deviation isn't an option—every action is mapped out, and unexpected inputs either halt the process or trigger manual intervention.

- **Real-World Example**: Consider an automated payroll system. It calculates salaries, deducts taxes, and issues payments in a set order. If an employee's hours aren't logged correctly, the workflow stalls until someone steps in to fix it.

Why Does It Matters?

- **AI Agents**: Thrive where independence is non-negotiable, adapting to the unknown without needing a babysitter.
- **Workflows**: Shine in controlled settings where consistency trumps flexibility.

Adaptability: Evolving Intelligence vs. Static Design

AI Agents: Built to Learn

AI agents don't just react—they **adapt**. Leveraging techniques like machine learning or reinforcement learning, they refine their behavior based on experience. This ability to evolve lets them tackle shifting priorities and novel challenges without human rewrites.

- **Real-World Example**: An AI-powered fraud detection system in banking starts with basic rules but grows smarter over time. As it encounters new fraud patterns—like a sudden spike in micro-transactions—it adjusts its thresholds and flags suspicious activity more accurately.

Workflows: Locked in Place

Workflows are **static** by nature. They execute the same steps, in the same way, until someone intervenes to update them. This rigidity ensures reliability but limits their ability to handle change without external effort.

- **Real-World Example**: A workflow for processing insurance claims checks predefined criteria (e.g., claim amount, policy type) and routes approvals accordingly. If a new regulation changes eligibility, the workflow stays oblivious until a programmer updates its rules.

Why Does It Matters?

- **AI Agents**: Excel in environments where learning from data or feedback is a game-changer.
- **Workflows**: Best for tasks where stability and repeatability outweigh the need for evolution.

Decision-Making: Strategic Reasoning vs. Simple Rules

AI Agents: Thinking Ahead

AI agents bring **reasoning and planning** to the table. They don't just follow instructions—they strategize, weighing options and predicting outcomes. This depth allows them to manage complex, multi-step challenges that demand foresight.

- **Real-World Example**: An AI agent managing a smart grid balances energy supply and demand. It forecasts usage spikes, reroutes power from solar farms or batteries, and optimizes for cost—all while avoiding blackouts. Each choice builds on a chain of calculated decisions.

28

Workflows: Sticking to the Script

Workflows lean on **rule-based logic**—think "if this, then that." They're efficient for simple, linear tasks but falter when nuance or context comes into play. Without the ability to reason beyond their programming, they're blind to anything not explicitly coded.

- **Real-World Example**: A workflow for inventory restocking checks stock levels against a threshold. If below 50 units, it triggers a reorder. It won't factor in seasonal trends or supplier delays unless those rules are hard-coded.

Why Does It Matters?

- **AI Agents**: Handle ambiguity and complexity with proactive decision-making.
- **Workflows**: Keep it simple, executing clear-cut rules with zero improvisation.

Use Cases: Matching Tools to Tasks

The choice between AI agents and workflows hinges on the problem at hand. Here's how their strengths align with real-world scenarios.

When AI Agents Excel

AI agents shine in **dynamic, unpredictable settings** where autonomy and adaptability are mission-critical. Their ability to perceive, decide, and adjust makes them indispensable in:

- **Logistics**: Autonomous forklifts in warehouses navigate crowded aisles, rerouting around spills or misplaced pallets while optimizing pickup sequences.
- **Healthcare**: AI agents interpret medical imaging, flagging anomalies in X-rays and suggesting follow-ups based on patient history—tasks too variable for rigid scripts.
- **Customer Experience**: Virtual assistants that personalize interactions, learning from user preferences to recommend products or troubleshoot issues proactively.
- **Security**: Threat detection systems that evolve with emerging cyberattack patterns, staying one step ahead of static defenses.

These scenarios demand systems that can think on their feet, not just follow a playbook.

When Workflows Suffice

Workflows are the go-to for **structured, repetitive processes** where predictability and ease of maintenance are priorities. They excel in:

- **HR Onboarding**: Automating steps like sending welcome emails, assigning training modules, and generating employee IDs—all linear and consistent.

- **E-commerce**: Processing orders from checkout to shipping, with fixed steps like payment verification and label generation.
- **Compliance**: Auditing expense submissions against company policies, flagging violations based on clear-cut rules.
- **Marketing**: Scheduling social media posts across platforms at set times, no improvisation needed.

In these cases, the task's stability makes workflows a lean, reliable choice.

Common Misconceptions: Separating Fact from Fiction

Misunderstandings often muddy the waters when comparing AI agents and workflows. Let's tackle the big ones head-on.

Misconception 1: Every Chatbot Is an AI Agent

The term "AI agent" gets thrown around loosely, especially with chatbots. Most chatbots, though, are **workflow-driven**, not true agents.

- **Workflow-Based Chatbot**: A customer asks, "Where's my order?" The system uses natural language processing (NLP) to identify the intent, then follows a script: check the order ID, pull tracking data, and reply. It's a fixed path with AI seasoning—not autonomy.
- **True AI Agent Chatbot**: Imagine a bot that notices a customer's frequent delays, proactively offers a discount, and

adjusts its tone based on past chats. It learns, decides, and acts independently—hallmarks of an agent.

How to Tell: If it's scripted and can't stray from the path without reprogramming, it's a workflow. True agents adapt and initiate without a leash.

Misconception 2: AI in a Workflow Makes It an Agent

Adding an AI tool—like an API for sentiment analysis—doesn't turn a workflow into an AI agent. The system might get smarter at one step, but if it still follows a rigid sequence, it's not autonomous.

- **Example**: A workflow emails customers based on survey responses. An AI scores the sentiment, but the email's timing and content are preset. No independence, no agent.

Misconception 3: Workflows Can't Handle Complexity

While workflows lack adaptability, they can manage intricate processes if the rules are well-defined. A multi-branch workflow with dozens of conditions isn't an agent—it's just a detailed script.

- **Example**: A loan approval workflow with checks for credit score, income, and debt ratio is complex but still rule-based.

Clearing the Fog

Ask these questions to classify a system:

- **Is it autonomous?** Agents act solo; workflows need guidance.
- **Does it learn?** Agents improve; workflows wait for updates.
- **Can it be the reason?** Agents plan; workflows obey.

5

Technical Deep Dive: Building AI Agents

Building AI agents is about creating systems that don't just follow instructions but perceive, reason, and act autonomously. This chapter explores the nuts and bolts of AI agent development: their architectures, the technologies that power them, the tools that simplify the process, and the challenges you'll face. We'll dive into cutting-edge concepts like **agentic Retrieval-Augmented Generation (RAG)**—a must-know for data-heavy applications—and examine how **decentralized blockchain** can ensure the integrity of the information agents rely on. To ground it all, we'll walk through a hands-on example of building a simple scheduling bot. Whether you're aiming for a basic goal-based agent or a sophisticated system for business or government, this ~4,000-word guide has you covered.

Architectures for AI Agents

An AI agent's architecture is its blueprint—how it senses its environment, makes decisions, and takes action. Two foundational models stand out: **Belief-Desire-Intention (BDI)** and **subsumption architecture**. Let's break them down.

Belief-Desire-Intention (BDI) Architecture

BDI is ideal for agents that need to pursue goals in complex, shifting environments. It's built on three core components:

- **Beliefs**: The agent's understanding of the world—its knowledge base, derived from data, sensors, or models.
- **Desires**: The objectives the agent wants to achieve, like completing a task or optimizing a process.
- **Intentions**: The concrete plans or actions the agent commits to, balancing its beliefs and desires.

Imagine a BDI agent as a strategist. It assesses the situation (beliefs), sets a target (desires), and executes a plan (intentions), adapting as new information arises.

- **Example**: A disaster response drone believes survivors are at coordinates A, B, and C, desires to save them all, and intends to prioritized the nearest location first. If a storm blocks its path, it reroutes based on updated beliefs.

Strength: BDI excels in dynamic settings where agents must juggle multiple goals and adjust on the fly.

Subsumption Architecture

Subsumption architecture takes a bottom-up approach, stacking simple behaviors into complex outcomes. Each layer handles a specific job, and higher layers can suppress or modify lower ones as needed. It's perfect for reactive, real-time systems.

- **How It Works**: Think of a robotic vacuum:
- Layer 1: Avoid walls and furniture.
- Layer 2: Roam the room randomly.
- Layer 3: Head to the dock when the battery's low.

There's no central decision-maker—just layered reflexes creating intelligent behavior.

- **Example**: Autonomous cars use subsumption with layers for staying in lanes, stopping for obstacles, and following navigation routes.

Strength: Subsumption delivers speed and robustness for systems that can't afford delays.

Which Architecture Wins?

- **BDI**: Choose it for goal-driven agents in unpredictable environments, like virtual assistants or logistics planners.
- **Subsumption**: Opt for it in reactive systems needing instant responses, like robots or IoT devices.

Technologies Powering AI Agents

AI agents lean on a tech stack to process information, make decisions, and act. Here's what drives them:

Machine Learning (ML)

ML gives agents the ability to learn and improve without explicit programming. It's the engine for adaptive behavior.

- **Supervised Learning**: Maps inputs to outputs—great for agents classifying data, like sorting emails into "urgent" or "routine."
- **Unsupervised Learning**: Uncovers patterns in unlabeled data, ideal for clustering customers or detecting anomalies.
- **Reinforcement Learning (RL)**: Teaches agents through rewards and penalties. RL shines in dynamic scenarios where trial and error builds expertise.
- **Example**: RL drives AlphaGo, which mastered the game of Go by simulating millions of matches and optimizing its moves.

Planning Algorithms

Planning algorithms help agents chart a course to their goals, especially when thinking ahead is critical.

- *A Search**: Finds the shortest path in a graph—think GPS routing or robot navigation.
- **Monte Carlo Tree Search (MCTS)**: Weighs exploration versus exploitation, perfect for decisions under uncertainty.

- **Example**: MCTS guides a delivery drone to pick routes avoiding weather hazards while minimizing energy use.

Agentic Retrieval-Augmented Generation (RAG)

For data-intensive tasks—common in business and government—**RAG** supercharges AI agents by blending large language models (LLMs) with real-time data retrieval.

- **Basic RAG**: The agent queries a database (e.g., company records or public laws), retrieves relevant documents, and feeds them to an LLM to generate a response or action. It's simple and effective for static knowledge tasks.
- **Use Case**: A customer service bot retrieves product manuals to answer queries accurately.
- **Agentic RAG**: Adds autonomy. The agent decides when to fetch data, what sources to trust, and how to act on it, adapting to its goals and context.
- **Use Case**: A government compliance agent pulls the latest regulations, assesses a citizen's request, and drafts a tailored, legally sound reply.
- **Why It Matters**: RAG keeps agents current without retraining, crucial for fast-evolving domains like finance, healthcare, or policy.

Tools and Frameworks for Building AI Agents

You don't need to reinvent the wheel. These tools streamline agent development:

JADE (Java Agent DEvelopment Framework)

- **What It Is**: A robust platform for multi-agent systems, handling communication and coordination.
- **Best For**: Distributed software agents, like optimizing a supply chain across factories.

SPADE (Smart Python Agent Development Environment)

- **What It Is**: A Python-based framework for quick prototyping with asynchronous messaging.
- **Best For**: Real-time agents, such as chatbots or IoT controllers.

ROS (Robot Operating System)

- **What It Is**: A flexible ecosystem for robotic agents, offering hardware drivers, simulation, and more.
- **Best For**: Physical robots, from warehouse bots to self-driving cars.

Bonus Tools

- **LangChain**: Simplifies RAG-based agents with LLM integration.
- **AutoGen**: Builds collaborative or competitive conversa-

tional agents.

Challenges in Building AI Agents

Even with the right tools, hurdles remain. Here's how to navigate them:

Safety and Reliability

- **Issue**: Agents can err in high-stakes settings—imagine a medical bot misdiagnosing or a financial agent miscalculating.
- **Solution**: Add **human oversight** and test exhaustively. For RL, use **constrained optimization** to cap risky moves.

Uncertainty Handling

- **Issue**: Real life is noisy—sensors glitch, data's missing, outcomes aren't guaranteed.
- **Solution**: Equip agents with **Bayesian reasoning** for probabilities or **robust control** to manage chaos.

Scalability

- **Issue**: Bigger systems mean bigger complexity, especially with multiple agents.
- **Solution**: Go **modular** and use **distributed computing**. For multi-agent setups, try **coordination protocols** like auctions.

The Role of Decentralized Blockchain in AI Agents

Data integrity is a make-or-break factor for AI agents, especially in trust-sensitive fields like government or business. **Decentralized blockchain** steps in as a powerful ally, offering an immutable, transparent ledger to:

- **Secure Data**: Agents can access verified, tamper-proof records—think supply chain logs or legal contracts.
- **Boost Trust**: Logging decisions on-chain creates an auditable trail, proving an agent's reliability.
- **Enable Transactions**: Blockchain supports secure, decentralized exchanges, perfect for agents handling payments or agreements.
- **Example**: A government procurement agent uses blockchain to check supplier histories, record bids, and execute contracts—all with guaranteed accuracy. This builds a rock-solid reputation for delivering true, unbiased information.

Pairing blockchain with AI agents isn't just technical—it's a trust multiplier, making them indispensable in critical applications.

Step-by-Step Example: Building a Scheduling Bot

Let's build a **goal-based agent**: a scheduling bot that finds a meeting time for three people. We'll use Python for clarity.

Step 1: Define the Environment

- **Participants**: Alice, Bob, Charlie.
- **Availability**: Free 1-hour slots from 9 AM to 5 PM.
- **Goal**: Book a slot all three can attend.

Step 2: Set Beliefs

The agent's beliefs are the schedules:

```python
availability = {
    "Alice": [(9, 10), (11, 12), (14, 15)],
    "Bob": [(10, 11), (12, 13), (15, 16)],
    "Charlie": [(9, 10), (12, 13), (14, 15)]
}
```

Step 3: Define Desire

Find a common 1-hour slot—or suggest the next best option.

Step 4: Plan with Intentions

We'll intersect the schedules:

```python
def find_common_slot(availability):
    common_slots = set(availability["Alice"])
    for person in availability:
        common_slots &= set(availability[person])
    return list(common_slots)

common_slots = find_common_slot(availability)
```

Step 5: Act

Book if possible, or propose an alternative:

```python
if common_slots:
    print(f"Booked: {common_slots[0]}")
else:
    all_slots = [slot for slots in availability.values() for slot in slots]
    best_slot = max(set(all_slots), key=all_slots.count)
    print(f"No common slot. Suggest: {best_slot}")
```

Step 6: Add Adaptability

Let's make it react to feedback:

```python
def suggest_slot(availability, rejected=[]):
    common_slots = find_common_slot(availability)
    if common_slots and common_slots[0] not in rejected:
        return common_slots[0]
    all_slots = [slot for slots in availability.values() for slot in slots if slot not in rejected]
    return max(set(all_slots), key=all_slots.count)

rejected = [(12, 13)]
print(f"Suggested: {suggest_slot(availability, rejected)}")
```

This bot now adapts, iterating based on rejections—a true agent trait.

6

Technical Deep Dive: Implementing Workflows with AI

Workflows are the heartbeat of automation, turning repetitive tasks into streamlined processes. When you infuse them with AI Large Language Models (LLMs), they evolve into something extraordinary—capable of generating content, analyzing data, or even chatting with customers. This chapter is your roadmap to building these AI-powered workflows. We'll explore **design principles** for scalable automation, show you how to integrate cutting-edge LLMs like **OpenAI GPT**, **Google Gemini**, **Anthropic Claude**, **xAI Grok**, and **DeepSeek**, and dive deep into tools like **Make**, **n8n**, **Zapier**, **Microsoft Power Automate**, and **Apache Airflow**. Plus, you'll get **best practices** and a hands-on example of an automated report generator. Let's get started!

Workflow Design Principles

A great workflow is like a perfectly tuned engine—smooth, adaptable, and reliable. Before we touch tools or APIs, here are the core principles to design one that lasts.

1. Define Clear Objectives

Know your goal from the start. Are you automating emails? Generating reports? One clear sentence sets the foundation.

- **Example**: "Create a workflow to summarize weekly sales data and email it to the team."

2. Map the Process

Break your task into steps. Each one is a piece of the puzzle—what happens first, next, and last?

- **Example Steps**:

1. Pull data from a CRM.
2. Format it for clarity.
3. Summarize it with an LLM.
4. Send it off via email.

3. Use Modularity

Keep steps independent. If one part changes—like switching CRMs—you won't need to rebuild everything.

- **Why**: Saves time and scales easily.

4. Incorporate Conditionals

Add "if-then" logic for flexibility. If data is missing, don't crash—adapt.

- **Example**: "If sales data is incomplete, notify the team instead of proceeding."

5. Plan for Errors

Things fail—APIs time out, inputs go wonky. Build in retries or alerts to keep things humming.

- **Tip**: Log errors for fast fixes.

Integrating AI LLM APIs

LLMs are the game-changers here, bringing intelligence to your workflows. Let's see how to plug in **OpenAI GPT**, **Google Gemini**, **Anthropic Claude**, **xAI Grok**, and **DeepSeek**.

Choosing the Right LLM

Each LLM shines in its own way:

- **OpenAI GPT**: The all-rounder—great for writing, summarizing, and chatting.

AI AGENTS VS WORKFLOWS

- **Google Gemini**: Built for speed and multimodal tasks (text, images, more).
- **Anthropic Claude**: Safety-first, perfect for sensitive or regulated uses.
- **xAI Grok**: Explainable AI, ideal for clarity in decision-making.
- **DeepSeek**: Deep learning focus, suited for technical or niche fields.

How to Choose: Need a creative blog post? Go GPT. Handling customer data securely? Claude's your pick.

How to Integrate LLMs

Most LLMs use REST APIs—here's the basic flow:

1. **Authenticate**: Grab an API key from the provider.
2. **Write a Prompt**: Tell the LLM what to do (e.g., "Summarize this data in 100 words").
3. **Send the Request**: Use an HTTP POST to hit the API.
4. **Use the Response**: Take the output and move it along.

Example: OpenAI GPT in Action

Imagine drafting automated email replies:

- **Trigger**: New customer email arrives.
- **Step**: Extract the query.
- **Prompt**: "Write a polite response to: [query]."
- **Output**: GPT drafts it, you send it.

Code Snippet (Python):

```python
import openai
openai.api_key = "your-api-key"
response = openai.Completion.create(
    model="gpt-4",
    prompt="Write a polite response to: " + query,
    max_tokens=150
)
reply = response.choices[0].text.strip()
```

Swap endpoints for Gemini, Claude, Grok, or DeepSeek—same idea, different flavor!

Tools for Workflow Automation

These tools are your canvas—some are no-code, others coder-friendly. Let's break down **Make**, **n8n**, and more.

Make (formerly Integromat)

- **What**: Drag-and-drop tool for complex, visual workflows.
- **Best For**: Multi-step tasks with logic (e.g., data cleaning + AI summarization).
- **AI Power**: Native modules for OpenAI, Google Gemini, and more—chain AI steps effortlessly.
- **Why It Rocks**: Intuitive yet powerful, perfect for intermediate users.

n8n

- **What**: Open-source, self-hosted automation for tech-savvy folks.
- **Best For**: Custom workflows with total control.
- **AI Power**: Nodes for OpenAI, Claude, and custom APIs—build what you dream.
- **Why It Rocks**: Free to start, endlessly tweakable.

Zapier

- **What**: No-code connector for apps via "Zaps."
- **Best For**: Simple tasks (e.g., Slack alerts from forms).
- **AI Power**: Supports OpenAI and Claude natively—add AI steps in clicks.

Microsoft Power Automate

- **What**: Enterprise-grade automation tied to Microsoft 365.
- **Best For**: Business tasks in Teams or SharePoint.
- **AI Power**: AI Builder + Azure OpenAI connectors.

Apache Airflow

- **What**: Code-based framework for heavy-duty workflows.
- **Best For**: Big data pipelines (e.g., ETL).
- **AI Power**: Python flexibility—call any LLM API.

Which Tool?

- **Beginners**: Zapier or Power Automate—no coding, quick wins.
- **Intermediate**: **Make** or **n8n**—balance of ease and power.
- **Pros**: Airflow—unlimited scale, total control.

Best Practices for AI-Enhanced Workflows

Build it right, and it'll run like a dream. Here's how:

1. Stay Modular

Reuse components. One summary template can serve multiple teams.

2. Optimize API Use

LLM calls cost money and time—batch requests or cache repeats.

- **Example**: Store common responses to skip redundant calls.

3. Handle Errors Smartly

Networks flake, APIs falter. Add retries or fallbacks.

- **Tip**: Retry with delays (exponential backoff) to avoid overload.

4. Monitor Everything

Log runs to catch hiccups. **Make** and **n8n** have built-in tracking.

5. Secure It

Encrypt sensitive data, hide API keys in variables—not code.

Example: Automated Report Generation Workflow

Let's build a real-world workflow using **Make** and **OpenAI GPT**: a weekly sales report emailed every Monday.

The Plan

Pull CRM data, clean it, summarize with GPT, and email it.

Step-by-Step

Trigger:

- **Tool**: Make.
- **Module**: Schedule—runs Monday, 8 AM.

Fetch Data:

- **Module**: HTTP Request.
- **Action**: Get last week's sales from CRM (e.g., Salesforce).

Clean Data:

- **Module**: Data Transformer.
- **Action**: Remove junk, format into JSON.

Summarize with GPT:

- **Module**: OpenAI GPT.
- **Prompt**: "Summarize this sales data in 3 bullet points: [data]."
- **Action**: Get the summary.

Send Email:

- **Module**: Email.
- **Action**: Send to sales team—"Weekly Sales Report."

Error Handling:

- **Module**: Error Handler.
- **Action**: Retry CRM call twice, then Slack admin if it fails.

Test & Launch:

- Test with fake data, check the summary, go live.

Turbocharge It

- Add "if sales > $10K, highlight it."
- Use **Google Gemini** for multilingual reports.

This workflow slashes manual effort, showing off AI's potential!

7

Case Studies

Theories and algorithms are fascinating, but nothing beats seeing technology in action. This chapter presents four case studies that demonstrate how AI agents and workflows solve real-world problems across diverse domains: transportation, customer service, home automation, and social media. Each case is dissected to reveal **why** a particular approach—AI agent or workflow—was chosen, **how** it works, and **what** makes it effective. From the chaotic streets navigated by self-driving cars to the structured efficiency of automated chatbots, these examples highlight the strengths of each method. Let's explore them one by one.

Case Study 1: AI Agent in Autonomous Vehicles

Technology: AI Agent (Goal-Based, Learning)
　Domain: Transportation
　Goal: Navigate from point A to point B safely and efficiently
　Word Count: ~750 words

Case Study 2: Workflow for Automated Customer Support

Technology: Workflow with LLM API
  Domain: Customer Service
  Goal: Resolve queries quickly and accurately
  Word Count: ~750 words

The Challenge

Customer support is a flood of questions—"Where's my package?" "Can I return this?"—and human agents can't keep up at scale. Businesses need a system that's fast, consistent, and cost-effective. A workflow-powered chatbot, using a large language model (LLM) API, steps up to handle the deluge while keeping quality high.

How It Works

The workflow follows a clear pipeline:

1. **Trigger**: A customer types a query into a chat window ("I need help with my bill").
2. **Intent Recognition**: An LLM API (like OpenAI's GPT) parses the text, identifying the intent—"billing issue"—with natural language understanding.
3. **Data Retrieval**: The system queries a database (e.g., billing records) to fetch relevant info—like the customer's latest invoice.
4. **Response Generation**: The LLM crafts a natural, precise reply: "Your bill of $45.32 was processed on October 10.

Need more details?".

5. **Escalation**: If the query stumps the system (e.g., "Why's my rate so high?"), it flags a human agent to step in.

Why a Workflow?

- **Efficiency**: It churns through thousands of queries hourly, no breaks needed.
- **Consistency**: Every "track my order" request gets the same reliable answer, avoiding human error or mood swings.
- **Scalability**: Adding new intents (e.g., "cancel subscription") is as simple as updating the workflow, no retraining required.

Effectiveness

- **Speed**: Tools like Zendesk's Answer Bot resolve 40% of inquiries instantly, cutting wait times to zero for routine issues.
- **Cost**: Automation reduces support costs by up to 30%, per industry reports, freeing humans for trickier cases.

Takeaway

Workflows shine in structured, repetitive tasks where speed and uniformity matter most. For customer support, they're a scalable lifeline that keeps satisfaction high and expenses low.

Case Study 3: AI Agent in Smart Home Systems

Technology: AI Agent (Learning, Utility-Based)
  Domain: Home Automation
  Goal: Optimize comfort, security, and energy efficiency
  Word Count: ~750 words

The Challenge

Smart homes manage a symphony of devices—thermostats, lights, locks—but static settings can't keep up with a family's quirks. An AI agent that learns and adapts can turn a house into a responsive, personalized haven.

How It Works

The agent operates across three stages:

- **Perception**: Sensors monitor the home—motion detectors spot activity, thermostats track temperature, and smart meters measure energy use.
- **Learning**: A utility-based agent analyzes patterns. It notices you crank the heat at 7 AM or dim lights at 9 PM, building a model of your preferences. Reinforcement learning refines its choices, maximizing a "utility score" of comfort and savings.
- **Action**: It acts proactively—preheating the house before you wake, locking doors when you leave, or shutting off unused lights.

Why an AI Agent?

- **Personalization**: It tailors settings to your habits, like brewing coffee when your alarm goes off.
- **Optimization**: It balances goals—keeping you cozy while trimming the electric bill.
- **Pro activity**: It anticipates needs, not just reacts, making life seamless.

Effectiveness

- **Convenience**: Google's Nest thermostat learns your schedule in a week, cutting energy use by 10-15%, per studies.
- **Security**: Ring's AI cameras reduce false alerts by 80%, distinguishing a cat from a burglar.

Takeaway

AI agents bring intelligence and flexibility to systems that need to evolve with users. In smart homes, they're the difference between a gadget-filled house and a truly responsive one.

Case Study 4: Workflow for Content Moderation

Technology: Workflow with AI Assistance
   Domain: Social Media
   Goal: Filter harmful content quickly and accurately
   Word Count: ~750 words

The Challenge

Social platforms face a tsunami of uploads—millions daily—some laced with hate speech or misinformation. Human moderators alone can't cope, but pure AI risks errors. A workflow blending AI and human oversight offers a balanced fix.

How It Works

The process unfolds in steps:

1. **Trigger**: A user posts a photo or comment.
2. **Pre-Screening**: An AI model scans for red flags—keywords, violent imagery—flagging potential issues in seconds.
3. **Human Review**: Moderators check flagged content, deciding if it violates policy.
4. **Action**: Safe posts go live; harmful ones are removed or sent for appeal.

Why a Workflow?

- **Consistency**: Defined steps ensure every post is judged by the same standards.
- **Transparency**: Human oversight keeps the process accountable, avoiding AI black-box pitfalls.
- **Efficiency**: AI handles the grunt work, letting humans focus on nuanced calls.

Effectiveness

- **Scale**: Facebook's AI flags 90% of hate speech preemptively, per its reports.
- **Accuracy**: Human-AI teams catch 95% of violations with fewer mistakes than solo automation.

Takeaway

Workflows, juiced by AI, tackle high-volume, rule-driven tasks with precision and fairness. For content moderation, they're the backbone of trust at scale.

Analysis: Why Each Approach Was Chosen

Word Count: ~500 words

These case studies spotlight a key insight: AI agents and workflows are tools for different jobs. Here's why each was picked and how it delivers.

AI Agents: When to Deploy

- **Dynamic Environments**: Self-driving cars face endless curveballs—traffic, weather, jaywalkers. Agents adapt on the fly, learning from each twist.
- **Personalization**: Smart homes mold to your life, tweaking settings as habits shift. Agents make it feel like the house knows you.
- **Strategic Decisions**: Agents weigh complex trade-offs—speed vs. safety, comfort vs. cost—making real-time calls

no static system could.

Effectiveness: Agents shine where flexibility and foresight are king. Tesla's crash stats and Nest's energy savings prove they handle chaos and customization like champs.

Workflows: When They Shine

- **Structured Tasks**: Customer support and moderation thrive on clear steps—parse, fetch, reply, or screen, review, act. Workflows nail repetition.
- **Scalability**: They process millions of inputs without blinking, from chat queries to posts.
- **Consistency**: Predictable outputs—same answer, same ruling—build trust and efficiency.

Effectiveness: Zendesk's 40% resolution rate and Facebook's 90% pre-flagging show workflows dominate where volume and reliability rule.

8

The Future of AI Agents and Workflows

The saga of AI agents and workflows has already reshaped our world, from self-driving marvels to seamless customer service bots. Yet, this is merely the prologue. The chapters yet unwritten promise a future of breathtaking advancements, intricate challenges, and profound opportunities. In this forward-looking adventure, we'll dive into how AI agents will sharpen their minds, how workflows will flex and evolve, and how together they'll redefine existence. With technical precision and a dash of visionary flair, here's what awaits us in the near and distant future.

Advancements in AI Agents

AI agents are poised for a leap into a new era, fueled by smarter algorithms, sharper decision-making, and a bolder presence in our physical world. Here's what's on the horizon:

1. Learning Algorithms: Beyond Boundaries

Today's AI agents are specialists—chess masters or navigation gurus—but tomorrow's will flirt with **general intelligence**, breaking free from narrow confines:

- **Meta-Learning**: Picture an agent that learns *how* to learn, mastering a new skill—like assembling furniture—after a single YouTube tutorial. This "learning to learn" will slash training times and broaden capabilities.
- **Transfer Learning**: Imagine a language-savvy agent applying its translation prowess to debug code or compose music. Skills will hop across domains, making agents wildly versatile.
- **Self-Supervised Learning**: No more hand-holding with labeled data—agents will sift through raw chaos, like a linguist decoding an alien tongue from scratch, spotting patterns where humans see noise.

2. Decision-Making: Seeing the Future

Forget reacting—future agents will predict and plan:

- **Causal Reasoning**: An agent diagnosing a patient won't just list symptoms; it'll unravel *why* they're happening—say, linking fatigue to a hidden infection—offering deeper insights.
- **Multi-Agent Coordination**: Think of drone swarms rebuilding a bridge, each unit anticipating the others' moves without a boss barking orders. Collaboration will be instinctive and elegant.

- **Explainable AI (XAI)**: Trust will soar as agents explain themselves. A loan-approval bot won't just say "no"—it'll detail why, empowering users to adjust and reapply.

3. Embodied AI: From Bits to Bodies

Agents will step out of the digital realm:

- **Robotics**: Humanoid helpers with nimble fingers and warm smiles will fold laundry or assist surgeries, blending into daily life.
- **Augmented Reality (AR)**: An AR agent might hover over your workbench, guiding you through a car repair with holographic pointers, turning novices into pros.

What to Expect: By 2035, AI agents will be as ubiquitous as smartphones—personalized companions that think, act, and adapt in ways we can scarcely imagine today.

Evolution of Workflows

Workflows—the unsung heroes of automation—are gearing up for a renaissance, weaving AI deeper into their fabric and embracing flexibility:

1. AI-Augmented Workflows

AI won't just tag along—it'll be the heartbeat:

- **Smart Routing**: A workflow handling customer complaints might spot a furious tone via an LLM and fast-track it to a human expert, skipping the usual hoops.

- **Generative Steps**: Need a report? An AI within the workflow will draft it, tweak it, and polish it—all in real time, turning rigid processes into creative allies.

2. Semi-Dynamic Workflows

Static scripts are out; adaptability is in:

- **Context-Aware Logic**: A shipping workflow might detour packages around a blizzard flagged by an AI weather model, keeping deliveries on track.
- **Human-AI Collaboration**: When a chatbot stumbles on a tricky query, the workflow will smoothly escalate it to a human, then learn from the handoff to improve next time.

3. No-Code Revolution

Workflow tools will become AI playgrounds:

- **Natural Language Design**: Say, "Email my team a sales update every Monday," and the platform builds it—no coding required.
- **Auto-Optimization**: Workflows will self-diagnose, trimming sluggish steps or suggesting shortcuts, like a chef refining a recipe mid-cook.

What to Expect: By 2030, workflows will run 50% leaner, with AI as their co-architect, making automation accessible to all.

Ethical Considerations

As AI agents and workflows flex their muscles, ethical shadows loom large. Here's what we'll grapple with—and how we might prevail:

1. Bias in AI Agents

Agents mirror their training data, and flawed data spells trouble:

- **Discriminatory Outcomes**: A recruitment agent might snub qualified candidates if past hires skewed male or urban.
- **Stereotype Amplification**: An LLM fed biased texts could churn out skewed narratives, entrenching old prejudices.

Solutions:

- **Diverse Datasets**: Feed agents a rich, balanced diet of data spanning cultures and contexts.
- **Bias Audits**: Regularly probe agents for fairness, tweaking algorithms to level the playing field.

2. Job Displacement from Automation

As workflows and agents take over, jobs will vanish:

- **Economic Shock**: Truckers, clerks, and factory workers could face layoffs as automation scales.
- **Skill Divide**: Demand for AI-savvy talent will spike, risking a chasm between the trained and the sidelined.

Solutions:

- **Reskilling Initiatives**: Fund programs to teach coding, AI oversight, or creative trades to displaced workers.
- **Safety Nets**: Experiments like Universal Basic Income (UBI) could ease the transition, giving people room to adapt.

3. Privacy and Surveillance

Always-on agents bring risks:

- **Data Overreach**: A home assistant tracking your habits might sell insights to marketers—or worse.
- **Security Gaps**: Hack an agent, and you've got a skeleton key to someone's life.

Solutions:

- **Minimalism**: Agents should hoard less data, keeping only what's vital.
- **Fortress-Level Security**: Encryption and regular updates will shield against breaches.

What to Expect: By 2027, ethics will dominate headlines and boardrooms, with laws demanding transparency and accountability from AI systems.

Societal Impacts

The waves from AI agents and workflows will crash across society, remaking how we work, learn, and heal:

1. Workforce Transformation

- **New Careers**: AI will birth roles like agent trainers, workflow architects, and ethics consultants, softening automation's blow.
- **Remote Work Unleashed**: Agents will juggle virtual schedules and draft docs, making distance irrelevant.
- **Gig Economy 2.0**: Agent-driven taxis or delivery drones will flood platforms, offering instant services with zero human fuss.

2. Education and Learning

- **Custom Tutors**: An AI agent will pace lessons to your quirks, turning a math-phobe into a calculus whiz.
- **Skill Evolution**: Workflows will scan job trends and nudge you toward hot courses, keeping you ahead of the curve.

3. Healthcare Revolution

- **Predictive Health**: Agents will watch your vitals, flagging risks—like a looming heart issue—before you feel a twinge.
- **Streamlined Systems**: Workflows will zap paperwork, letting doctors focus on healing, not filing.

What to Expect: By 2040, AI could stretch life expectancy by five years and shrink education gaps, leveling global playing fields.

Predictions for the Next Decade

Where are AI agents and workflows headed? Here's a timeline blending precision and possibility:

2025-2030: Convergence and Collaboration

- **Hybrid Powerhouses**: Workflows will sprout mini-agents for autonomous tasks—like a support pipeline with a bot to soothe angry callers—blurring their lines.
- **AI-as-a-Service**: Cloud platforms will peddle ready-made agents and workflows, letting startups punch above their weight.

2030-2040: Autonomy and Integration

- **Agent Ecosystems**: Agents will barter skills—like a traffic agent feeding data to a logistics bot—forming a buzzing digital marketplace.
- **Self-Evolving Workflows**: Armed with AI, workflows will rewrite themselves, shedding weak links based on real-time results.

Beyond 2040: The Edge of Imagination

- **Super intelligent Agents**: If general AI dawns, agents might outthink us, cracking climate puzzles or curing cancers in a flash.
- **Workflow Fadeout**: With agents ruling complexity, workflows could retire to niche roles, relics of a simpler age.

Wild Card: Quantum computing could ignite both, letting agents model galaxies or workflows orchestrate global supply chains in blinks.

9

Conclusion

As we reach the end of this exploration into AI agents and workflows, it's time to step back and reflect on the ground we've covered. We've journeyed through the technical depths of autonomy, adaptability, and decision-making, seen real-world applications from self-driving cars to automated customer support, and even peered into the future of these transformative technologies. Now, let's distill the essence of what sets AI agents and workflows apart, underscore why choosing the right tool matters, and look ahead to the role AI will play in shaping the world of automation. Finally, I'll leave you with a challenge— one that invites you to take these ideas from the page and into your own projects.

Recap of Key Differences

At the heart of this book lies a fundamental distinction: **AI agents** and **workflows** are two sides of the automation coin, each with unique strengths and purposes. Let's revisit their defining traits:

- **Autonomy**: AI agents are the trailblazers of independence.
  They perceive their environment, make decisions, and act
  without human intervention, thriving in the unpredictable.
  Workflows, by contrast, are the disciplined executors, following a predefined sequence of tasks with precision but
  little room for deviation.
- **Adaptability**: AI agents evolve. Through learning algorithms and real-time feedback, they refine their behavior,
  turning setbacks into stepping stones. Workflows remain
  static, requiring manual updates to handle new scenarios—
  a reliable but rigid companion.
- **Decision-Making**: AI agents think strategically, weighing
  options and planning ahead like a chess grandmaster. They
  navigate complexity with reasoning and foresight. Workflows, on the other hand, operate on rule-based logic—
  efficient for routine tasks but blind to nuance beyond their
  script.

These differences aren't just academic; they're the compass for
choosing the right tool. Imagine trying to navigate a stormy
sea with a map that never changes—workflows excel on calm
waters, but AI agents are built for the tempest.

Importance of Choosing the Right Approach

In the world of automation, the right tool isn't just a
preference—it's a necessity. Misapplying AI agents or
workflows can lead to inefficiency, frustration, and missed

opportunities. Think of it like choosing between a Swiss Army knife and a scalpel: both are sharp, but only one is suited for surgery.

- **When to Choose AI Agents**: If your problem is dynamic, unpredictable, or requires learning from experience, an AI agent is your ally. Whether it's a self-driving car dodging pedestrians or a smart thermostat adjusting to your habits, agents shine where autonomy and adaptability are non-negotiable.
- **When to Choose Workflows**: For structured, repetitive tasks—think processing payroll or moderating social media posts—workflows are the gold standard. They deliver speed, consistency, and scalability without the overhead of building intelligence.

The stakes are high. A workflow in a chaotic environment is like a train without tracks—it derails fast. An AI agent in a simple, rule-based task is overkill, like using a supercomputer to add two numbers. The art lies in matching the tool to the task, ensuring your automation efforts are as effective as they are efficient.

Final Thoughts: The Future Role of AI in Automation

As we look to the horizon, the future of AI in automation is both thrilling and humbling. AI agents and workflows are set to evolve in tandem, each pushing the boundaries of what's possible:

76

- **AI Agents** will inch closer to general intelligence, becoming more versatile, collaborative, and even empathetic. Imagine agents that not only manage your schedule but anticipate your needs, or robots that don't just assemble cars but design them.
- **Workflows** will grow smarter, integrating AI to handle exceptions and optimize themselves. They'll remain the backbone of business processes, but with newfound flexibility—think workflows that rewrite their own rules based on real-time data.

Yet, this future isn't without its shadows. Ethical dilemmas—bias, privacy, job displacement—will demand our vigilance. The challenge isn't just building smarter systems but ensuring they serve humanity's best interests. As AI reshapes industries, education, and healthcare, it will be up to us to steer its course, balancing innovation with responsibility.

Still, the promise outweighs the peril. In a world where AI agents and workflows coexist, we stand to unlock unprecedented levels of productivity, creativity, and human potential. The automation revolution is not about replacing us—it's about amplifying what we can achieve.

Call to Action: Your Turn to Build

Now, it's your turn. You've seen the blueprints, studied the case studies, and glimpsed the future. But knowledge without action is like a car without fuel—it won't get you far. I challenge you to take the next step: **experiment with AI agents and workflows in your own projects**.

- **Start Small**: Build a simple workflow to automate a daily task—perhaps a Zapier automation to organize your inbox. Then, try your hand at a basic AI agent—maybe a Python script that learns to play tic-tac-toe.
- **Think Big**: As you grow comfortable, scale up. Could an AI agent optimize your team's workflow? Could a workflow streamline data processing in your business? The possibilities are as vast as your imagination.
- **Stay Curious**: Dive into the tools we've discussed—JADE, SPADE, ROS for agents; Zapier, Make, n8n for workflows. Explore the LLMs from OpenAI, Google, and beyond. The best way to learn is by doing.

Remember, the future of automation isn't reserved for tech giants or research labs—it's in your hands. Whether you're a developer, a business leader, or a curious tinkerer, you have the power to shape how these technologies unfold. So, go forth, build, break, and rebuild. The world needs your creativity, your questions, and your solutions.

Automation is no longer a distant dream—it's here, and it's yours to command.

About the Author

Orion Bit is a distinguished technology expert with over a decade of blockchain expertise, more than two decades in ICT, and over three years specializing in AI implementation. As a trusted advisor and consultant, he helps businesses and governments harness cutting-edge technologies to drive efficiency, growth, and success through his expert solutions.

With a **Law Degree (LLB with Honours)** from a prestigious university, Orion brings a unique blend of legal insight and technological expertise to the rapidly evolving digital landscape. This distinctive background allows him to navigate complex regulatory frameworks while ensuring compliant and strategic technology adoption.

Known for simplifying complex concepts, Orion is passionate about empowering professionals to thrive in our technology-driven world. Through his expert solutions, consulting work and writing, he shares practical strategies and insights that help readers effectively leverage blockchain and AI for business advancement.

Orion's mission is to bridge the gap between emerging technologies and real-world applications, making innovation accessible and actionable for organizations through his expert solutions.